The Start of a

Healing
Conversation

An Approach to Healing a People Who Have Been:
Uprooted, Disconnected, Disjointed, and
Dehumanized by the System of Slavery in America

By Edgar Gosa

Heart Thoughts Publishing
Floyds Knobs, Indiana

Printed in the United States of America

First Printing, 2013

ISBN-13: 978-1492282877
ISBN-10: 1492282871

LCCN: 2013949257

Heart Thoughts Publishing
P.O. Box 536
Floyds Knobs, IN 47119

Comments About "The Start of a Healing Conversation"

As I read "Healing Conversation," I reflected on the times grandparents were able to be grandparents and neighbors were able to be neighbors, realizing, it takes a village to raise a child; a time, when if you failed to do what you were taught and what was expected of you, every adult who noticed your wrong, became your parent, not because they birth you into this world, but because that is who we are as a people. "Healing Conversation," addresses the need for inner healing in our community to take place, from every perspective of who we are as a people; physically, mentally and spiritually. Every part of us, as a person as well as a people, must come together to help our society to heal, and become healthy and be made whole again. Further, Brother Gosa acknowledges that we must have a connection with God in our lives as well. As painful as it is to face our failures, I am grateful that Brother Gosa opened this discussion so that the healing may begin. I am sure, that as you read this book, you will be able to reflect on who you are and how your personal contributions, can make our community better, one bite at a time!

Pastor Schmetrice Hughes-Bell
Pastor of Spiritual Awakening Church of Holiness; Northeastern Illinois Graduate; Senior Tax Accountant

To begin healing, we are grateful to Edgar for inspiring us to begin on this healing journey. I strongly thank him for giving us the impetus now. Because of his motivation and because of the long journey to healing ahead of us, let's talk!

Father George Clements
Former Priest of Holy Angels Catholic Church

Edgar is a God-fearing and inspired man. This writing reflects a lifestyle and commitment to humanity that commands spiritual growth through honest, truthful conversation.

Howard Saffold
Former Chicago Police Officer; A Founding Member, and Past President of the Afro American Police League; Coordinator of Security for Mayor Harold Washington

Ed, thank you for directing us away from solutionless arguments about causes, to our place at the table, to engage in a meaningful discussion about the cure. The question for each of us is; "Are you willing to participate?" It begins with a Healing Conversation and willing hearts. We are free to choose. We must be responsible to God and one another. Let's talk.

Rev. Robert Ervin
Former Chicago Police Officer, Board Member Afro-American Police League; Funeral Business Executive

Ed, I commend and salute you on this outstanding presentation. I think the frame of references presented chronicles our sojourn here in North America. It's quite illuminating indeed. Your incisive analysis of the historical, systemic and social implications of our struggle and trek is very revealing. You offer penetrating insight into the many complexities undergirding much of our present circumstances. It is a must read by all of us who fervently seek and hope for a better future.

Wilbourne Woods
Former Chicago Police Officer, Member of the Afro American Police League; Graduate Student - Roosevelt University

In "The Healing Conversation," Brother Ed outlines a viable process of how we can come together to begin a much need dialogue that must lead to plans for action toward liberation and freedom. He points out that central to developing a successful healing process, it is imperative that we draw from a spiritual power that is greater than ourselves. In doing so, the spirit of love will emanate, thus the environment for us to regain the true memory of who we are will manifest; "For without memory, lies are believed." We must become entrenched in the process of healing, in order to purge the lies about who we believe ourselves to be. The truth will set us free and liberate us.

Pat Hill
Retired Chicago Police Officer; President, Executive Director of the African America Police League Educator; Master of Science Degree, Law Enforcement Administration

Uncle Ed, your moral soundness, honesty, freedom from self-corruption, your self-respect and your sense of values, brings harmony and adds a component of integrity to the healing conversation.

Bill Gosa
Professional Photographer and Collage Professor

Acknowledgments

First, I acknowledge God, to whom all praise is due, forever and ever.

In line next, is my mother, Emma Jeanie and of course my father George Washington, for their role in my entering into this world. I will forever be grateful to them for their cooperation in providing me with the opportunity to be here. I am their last born of twelve children. My parents were mature in age when I was conceived. I have been blessed to have grown up in a wonderful, wholesome, and caring family environment. Family has been the foundation of my life's existence, from birth to maturity.

I also must thank my sister, Sophia, who reared and cared for me since the age of four following my mother's death.

I want to thank my childhood sweetheart, Pearl, who has been there for me with love and support for many years. We have been blessed with three marvelous children, Edgar II, Gina and Angie. I must thank them as well, for being great and wonderful children, never causing us any difficulties.

There is my Goddaughter, Melody and her husband Andre, who are most appreciated for all the many ways they have made contributions in my life.

Then, there is my nephew Bill, the son of my oldest brother. Bill has been a tremendous encouragement to me in the last few years.

I served time in the military, which opened up my life's horizons. Following my military time, I served thirty years in the Chicago Police Department. During that time, I connected with a group of Policemen who formed the African American Police League. Those that I worked closely with were Renault, Howard, Jack aka Hodari, Frank, Ocie, Ronald, Robert, Jerry, Albert, Charles, Wilborn, Jimmy, Phillip, Ray, Tony, Tom, Dave, Deloris, Ida, Jackie, and Patricia. There are many other members whose names are too numerous to name at this time, but suffice it to say, they all have played a role in my life. As I venture into this healing conversation, I want them to know that I love and appreciate them all and I thank them for being there in a time of need.

There are others, who are non-police and non-blood family members who are just as significant to this conversation as the others. I cannot forget to acknowledge my son-in-law Mike. He and I have had many conversations on this subject. I need to mention my friend W.L Lillard who helped me get focused during a trying period in my life.

Lastly, I want to thank my spiritual overseer, Minister Mary Agee, and my pastor, Minister Schmetrice Hughes-Bell who have helped me to focus my mind and heart spiritually, as a member of Spiritual Awakening Church of Holiness.

All-in-all, I end where I began, with God, who is the source of it all. Amen

Table of Contents

Preface

This conversation is for those of us who live in the African American community of Chicago, Illinois, and for every African American community all over the United States of America. This is also for every African on and from the continent of Africa. Our continued existence as a people of moral and noble character depends on our people being healed from this sick and diseased state of affairs that we are presently in. We must begin to engage in frank and honest dialogue about what is happening with our people in our communities that is causing them to be in this present condition of destruction and mayhem. We need this healing conversation in order for us to rescue ourselves from this intrusion of confusion and this invasion of contamination from outside forces into the psyche of our people, that has caused us to lose sight of who we are. We have a choice to make. Do we continue down the path we're on now, which is a path of self-destruction or change the paradigm? We must challenge ourselves to have dialogue that will lead us to a path of reunification as a people; we must address and repair the damage caused by the Slave Trade and the System of Slavery in America. It's a matter of individual and collective preservation.

We have been able to survive the many atrocities that were heaped upon us over the years, because of the persistence of our Ancestors. They recognized the spiritual nature of our creation, and had a deep love and respect for all of life. They passed this tradition on through customs, culture and ritual, to succeeding generations, that served as a foundation of personal and group strength. The traditions of our ancestors had a unifying and harmonizing effect on us; individually and collectively. It carried us for generations and generations, before the Europeans arrived on the continent and disrupted the continuity of this tradition.

This source of strength which was provided by the traditions of our ancestors was deeply rooted in love and a healthy respect for life. It has grown weak today due to the many years of intrusion of confusion and invasion of contamination in the cultural psyche and spiritual nature of our people from external forces. Our grandparents, great-grandparents, and great-great grandparents endured humiliating and devastating psyche and spiritual degradation during their encounter with the slavery experience. These pioneers who were captured Africans of the Slave Trade and the system of chattel slavery, perpetuated by "white supremacy - black inferiority," which was kept alive by violence and cruelty and through the advent of laws called "Jim

Crow Laws" and upheld by the court system of this country.

Our ancestors were outlawed and prohibited by the Slave System in America to engage in rituals and culture traditions. Our traditional culture has been all but forgotten. The absence of these rituals and cultural expressions and the continued re-enforcement of love which they provided for many generations are now non-existing and the energy of the human spirit, in some of our people, in particular, some of our boys and young men, is now manifesting in an ugly way. In some of our youth there is an absence of love for one another and a total disrespect for life. Killing and dying seems to have become the order of the day.

Slavery cut us away from our source of strength of who we were. "White Supremacy" and "Jim Crow" have had a devastating effect on the psyche of our people. Understanding the psychological impact of slavery in this healing conversation is critical to our continued survival as a people and thus, must be a significant part of the healing conversation. We must face the demon head-on so that we can rescue ourselves from what is happening in our communities on a daily basis. We must have this conversation to help us and our children find our way back home. It's a matter of survival.

Introduction

Living in the African American community has snares of all kinds and many stressful contributors, affecting the people in a multitude of ways such as:

- Causing health issues for individuals that manifest in all manner of illnesses.

- Causing inappropriate and unhealthy behaviors among the people in the community such as:

  - Babies being born without the comfort of a two parent home, which consists of a father and mother.

  - Soaring unemployment among the men and women of the community.

  - Young and old men, sitting, walking and standing around on the block committing muggings, robberies, burglaries, thefts, rapes, shootings, home invasions, causing fear and terror in neighborhoods.

  - Arguing, fussing and fighting seems to have become a way of life.

  - The police are stopping drivers of cars, jacking them and their passengers upside the car, searching them and tearing the inside of cars apart. They are stopping and searching people as they walk to and fro down the streets as well. Our boys and young men are their favorite targets.

This has become the norm; we have accepted this as the way to live, so it seems. It's just so much stuff, what are we to do? I don't know about you, but I'm sick and tired of it, and I'm sick and tired of being sick and tired. To me, this sounds and looks like a community that is sick, in pain, and in need of healing.

Let's have a healing conversation.

How it Began

My friends and I, who are retired and present Chicago Police Officers, were at a meeting the other day talking about the newly elected mayor of Chicago and the newly appointed Superintendent of The Chicago Police Department. We were discussing such concerns as;

- What will they do to affect crime and violence in the black community?

- What impact will their actions have on the youth and the young men of the community?

- What do we or what can we do about what's happening in the community?

- How can we change the incidents of crime, violence and killings in the black community?

- What can we do to help people who are coming back into the community after a stint in prison, with that proverbial "X" on their back?

This group is having a hard time in a society that won't give or allow them an opportunity to do something positive and be productive in the community. Employment for this group, who are mostly men, is almost none existing. Our conversation also included Michelle Alexander's new book, "The New Jim Crow." We talked about many things of this nature; all of which led to the discussion about a community that's in need of healing.

A few days later, my son-in-law and I were riding down the street, talking and listening to talk radio, WVON. The conversations on the radio were all about problems in the Black community. The show discussed problems with black folks, complaints about what's wrong, and the things that are affecting the African American community. This show also mentioned how President Barack Obama, our first African American president, is being treated with so much disdain and disrespect. Complaints, complaints, complaints. Each complaint was about the negative aspects of the black community. There was very little discussion about the positive aspects of the community or providing workable solutions to the ills and aliments that are causing the problems. The conversation was a full dose of the "ills," "ailments," and "the blues" of our community. It was apparent from this radio program; we are a community that is in need of having a healing conversation.

It was also apparent that the healing conversation needed to cover a multitude of topics. It has to be real with no sugar coating. We must have meaningful discussions about:

- Single family homes, where women are raising children without the involvement of a male partner

- Resources to help children develop and be successful

- The perceived schism between the Black male and the Black female

- High unemployment rates among black men

- Integration

- White supremacy - Black inferiority

- Slavery

- Sin, disobedience and being out of harmony with God's will and plan

The list goes on. The conversations that I had with my friends and son-in-law, coupled with my love and concern for Black People, African people, and all people if you will, has inspired me to write this book about the need for the Black community to have a healing conversation. Let's begin.

What does it mean "To Heal"?

When asked the question, where does healing begin; the answer is always the same, at the beginning of having health. So for this conversation, the beginning is knowing and understanding the meaning of "health." Health is a state of well-being. Health, as referenced in Webster's New Universal Unabridged Dictionary, means;

- Physical and mental well-being

- Soundness

- Freedom from defect, pain, or disease

- Normality of mental and physical functions.

Health is something different from strength, so don't be confused. The word "heal" also relates to "health," so we need to understand this word as well. Heal means, as referenced in Webster's New Universal Unabridged Dictionary;

- to make whole

- to make sound, well, or healthy again; restore to health

- to cure or get rid of; restore

- to free from grief, troubles, evil, etc.

- to remedy or get rid of

- to make up (a breach, a differences, etc.) to reconcile

Synonyms include cure, remedy, and restore.

So with this backdrop of understanding health and healing and along with what we see, hear and know about what happens every day in our communities and neighborhoods, we know that the community is in need of healing. So when I speak of healing, I'm talking about making the community well, whole, sound, and healthy again. In order to accomplish this, there must be some type of diagnosis; an analysis of the disease or disorder, if you will, to frame the healing conversation. There is no question that something is wrong, but what is it? When you speak of healing, the question is usually, "Healing from what, to what?"

Well, when we look at what is happening in the community as it relates to the violence, killings, destruction, drugs, lawlessness, etc., it's all about what people in the community are doing; it's about the action or behavior of these people. We have a community in which too many of its people are out of control. They behave like a community of thugs, criminals, gangsters and drug dealers. We must cause our people to see ourselves, in a different light. When we view ourselves as thugs, then we act like thugs, and we do what they do; they rob, steal, and kill. This is the kind of acts of behavior that must be healed in our community.

Heredity, Genetics or Destiny?

I start the healing conversation with these questions. Is it hereditary or just the nature of Black people? Is there a genetic disposition for Black people to behave like this or are there other factors? Have Black folks always been this way? Are we destined to act and treat one another the way we do now?

I think not. I know of a time when things were different. I can remember when we cared for each other. We looked out for one another. We respected ourselves and others. We respected our women and children. We cared for and protected our elderly, our children, and our women. We glorified life. What happened? What went wrong?

Well, a lot of things happened, and a lot of things went wrong. There is no quick fix, there's no one stop solution, but I do know this, it has to start with an honest and focused conversation about the need for healing; healing for this uprooted, disconnected, disjointed, and dehumanized community of people.

If all you know is that you're here, and don't know how you got here, where you came from, and you don't know where you're going, you are lost. That's why it's so important that we have this conversation; to find our way back home to a healthy state of being, individually and collective, and as a community.

When I say that the community needs healing, let's be clear. I am talking about the place where people live, and carry out their daily activities and functions. It's a geographical area with physical structures called homes, where the people make their abode.

Then, there are other structures that are used to carry out business activities, called stores. These physical structures in some community areas are fine and well, and in other community areas, not so fine and well. However, these structures or buildings are the way that they are due to the actions and behavior of the people who live and function there. So the condition of the buildings is the results of people who live and function within those communities. The focus of our healing must be on the people of the community not the physical homes and stores in that community. If we heal the people, the physical structures in the community will be alright.

We Are Sick. What's the Cure?

In this discussion, we have identified the people with anti-social, criminal and destructive behavior, who live in the community as the patient, not the physical structures of the community that need to be healed. So this healing conversation is about, people and their behavior; the actions of some and/or the inaction of others. This includes our own actions which we need to look at as well and address in this healing conversation.

Why is this point so important? I make this point because I want the focus to be on the people, not stuff and things. Stuff and things are the results of the decisions people make and about what they do with stuff and things. We must focus on a cure for the people, "not stuff and things." So then, the healing conversation must start with talking about the action or behavior of the people, to bring about the proper restoration or healing to the community.

Take a look at the prescription for healing; cure, remedy, and restore. I will start the discussion with the cure. What is the cure? Changing the actions and behavior of out of control people is the cure. The action and behavior of out of control people have been identified as the disease or disorder that's causing the need for this healing conversation. What's the prescription?

Prescription For the Cure

The action and behavior of a person starts with making a decision, so my focus of a cure will start with decision making. The following is my understanding of decision making.

Decision making starts with wanting to say something, do something, or cause something to happen. But first we must weigh the results, outcome or consequences. We assess or evaluate the outcome or consequences of what we are about to say, do, or cause to happen, BEFORE any action or behavior takes place. We need to know if it will be a good thing or a bad thing, something positive or negative, beneficial and helpful or harmful and hurtful. We must ask ourselves what affect our decision will have. How will it affect us and our lives or someone else and their life?

If everything lines up with a positive, good, helpful, happy and pleasurable effect on us and our life and the same for someone else and their life, then we can conclude that the likelihood of the decision we are about to make is alright. The prescription for the cure of a community in need of healing is making better choices and decisions.

Applying TAR to the Situation

There is another aspect of decision making that is important to know about and understand. It is called thinking, analyzing, or reasoning; what I like to refer to as TAR. This was alluded to earlier in this conversation when I mentioned the things I do while getting ready to make a decision. First I have a brief conversation with myself. I weigh the possible outcomes or conclusions of the decision I'm about make. This aspect of the decision requires one to have some related information and/or prior knowledge about the acceptable or desired outcome and conclusion of the decision one is about to make, not just ones feelings or emotions. This is where so many people are getting trapped, in their feelings and emotions. This is an area that needs plenty of attention. This is an area that requires the individual person to reach out for self-help and self-development in one's related intellectual and reasoning aspect of their decision making.

The role of the healing conversation is to raise the awareness and consciousness level of our people in our actions, behavior, and in our relationships with one another. We can then have a loving and compassionate relationship with each other and rid ourselves of the hate and condemnation attitude that is so prevalent and running rampant in the community. We must make better decisions for us to have a better community.

Physical and Relationship Health

In addition to looking at how we make decisions, we need to experience a conscious, collective, internal identity with each other, which will cause us to relate to one another as brothers and sisters. We must understand that we are a family in order for the community to heal. This speaks to the spirit of love as a component of the healing conversation.

There is another aspect of healing that should be mentioned as a part of the healing conversation. This one relates to the wellness of our individual physical bodies, which relates to our overall health. We must give personal attention to issues such as high blood pressure, diabetes, high cholesterol, heart problems, etc. African Americans in this country are plagued with a myriad of medical health conditions that primarily has to do what and the way we eat. We are plagued with a number of stress factors in our lives. This may seem like more of a personal health matter than a collective community issue to address, but it is not. Each member of the community is important and has a vital role to play. When members of the community are not able to effectively fulfill their roles, it affects the entire community. Nutrition, mental and physical health issues are matters that need to be addressed in this healing conversation.

Getting Back on Track

How and where did we get off track? Where did we go wrong? Like I mentioned earlier in the conversation, a lot of things went wrong that caused us to get off track. Many things went into supporting what happened. There is no quick fix and there is no one-stop solution. However, there must be an ongoing healing conversation, not just complaining about the problems. We must talk about solutions and take action that will heal us and make us a whole and complete people again. We must engage in a compressive account of what went wrong, or what happened that got us off track for healing to occur.

We have to challenge ourselves and one another to engage in research and study, so that we can identify what went wrong. We must thoroughly investigate what happened to get us off track, and has caused us to end up in this condition and to engage in this inhumane and anti-social behavior that our community is now experiencing. We must change this inhuman and antisocial way we relate to each other. This is something that we must do for ourselves, individually and collectively as a people. It is better that the remedy comes from within the community than for it to come from someone that is not of the community.

External forces do not have the kind of compassion and concern for the people as we should have. These are our people, our children, our brothers and sisters, our aunts, uncles, and cousins. This is our family. As the community represents our extended family, this includes our neighbors and friends.

I don't want to be looked upon as some crazy alarmist. But, the way I see it, if we continue down the path we're on, we will become extinct as a people. Too many of our people, particularly our youth, are clueless as to the effect of their actions which are causing us as a community of people to be off track. Too many adults have adopted a hands-off approach, and others have joined in with the young folk with an attitude, "if you can't beat em, join em." Wrong, wrong, wrong! We must teach them and show them the way.

The people of the community will not and cannot heal by using Gestapo type police methods that occurs now. The community cannot be healed by imposing five-hundred dollars fines on parents for their children curfew violations. These are the kinds of tactics that come from forces outside of the community. They sound good perhaps, but they really add to the problem. Do we really want to turn our family and friends over to this type of intrusion? I think not, but that's exactly where we're headed.

Read the "The New Jim Crow" by Michelle Alexander. She talks about the massive arrest number of Black folk, particularly black males, and how individual rights and their lives are being affected. Truth be told, life in our whole community is being affected; families are being destroyed, communities are being impacted. What affects one, affects us all, negatively or positively. This is a principal of the universe.

We Are God's People and People of Africa

I strongly believe that we must look at the spiritual aspect of this issue in order to begin to get back on track. I accept that I'm being inspired by God concerning this healing conversation and about what to say in this conversation. Whatever you want to call the ultimate source of creation; God, Spirit, the Source or the Absolute, it doesn't matter to me. However, as a people, spirituality is a key to this discussion. African Americans are descendants of a people that are highly spiritual; they are people of God. I reference this scripture:

If my people, which are called by my name, shall humble themselves, and pray, and seek my face, and turn from their wicked ways; then will I hear from heaven, and will forgive their sin, and will heal their land.

2 Chronicles 7:14

African Americans' ancestral homeland was invaded by hostile forces. They were uprooted from their homeland; disconnected from their family and village; disjointed from caring about or love for one another; dehumanized and made into chattel slaves, owned as personal property. That has caused us to be a confused people. We have forgotten and lost our identity of who we are, we have lost collective relationship with God. We have forgotten that we are God's chosen people, a people who were a loving and caring people, respecting all of creation. We are now a people who are puffed-up with "me-ism," "I-ism," and the like. We need to humble ourselves, return to an identity and relationship with God, turn from our wicked ways, and connect to our spirituality and love for us to be healed. My conversation is not about religion or the church, but how we are to relate to God and each other, in the spirit of love and in truth.

> *Beloved, let us love one another: for love is of God; and every one that loveth is born of God, and knoweth God. He that loveth not knoweth not God; for God is love.*
>
> *1 John 4:7-8*

I make reference to scripture in this conversation because I want to direct the focus toward the words of the scripture, so that we can enlist the power and the Spirit of the words presented in the scripture. It is not about the King James translation or some notion of religious belief. It is about the pure energy of the Word of God, without any biases or hang-ups. I'm talking about our decision that affects our relationship with God.

This conversation is not about the "Bible," the "Church," or "religion." The focus here is on the Word of God, which I relate to it as the "Book of Instruction." It tells us to have love for one another. I lay claim that this is part of the problem in the African American community. Black people have gotten away from the love for each other. When we fail to love one another, it becomes the source of our illness that affects the identity, association, and relationship with each other.

We dismiss God as the "god" of someone else's religion, not the source of our creation and our spiritual foundation. When we do this we dismiss the source of our strength; we have lost our identity of who we were.

We operate from the foundation of physical and mental slavery in America, a system of slavery that uprooted a people from a homeland base, disconnected them from a people base; disjointed them from a loving and caring human relationships rooted in God, forced into a system of slavery and white supremacy, black inferiority society existence. This situation and condition has not had proper remedial attention. We are in virtual slavery even now.

There are two major areas of concern that I have relating to this conversation about a community that needs healing. Both areas of concern have to do with "identity." When I speak of "identity," I want it to be understood that our identity is of two natures, an identity of a spiritual nature and an identity of a physical nature. It is important that we have some knowledge and some understanding of both.

In my opinion, we must know and accept that we are created in the image and the likeness of God, which is spirit and we are physical beings with a specific physical identity. We are constructed and constituted the same as every other human being on the planet, no lessor or no greater. We are not an inferior people based on skin pigmentation nor is anyone superior based the lack of skin pigmentation. We excel or we fail by what we do or don't do. What makes a people great is not the color of their skin, but content of their character and what they do; their actions and their behavior individually and collectively. We have attributes and gifts that make us who we are. We must seek to develop these things for the betterment of ourselves and of the collective whole once again. We were builders and inventors of phenomenal things, inspired by God. That's why it's so important for us to recognize and have a relationship with God in our everyday life.

The Bible says God is Spirit and God is Love. The Bible has this to say about how we are to be:

God is a Spirit: and they that worship him must worship him in spirit and in truth.
                              John 4:24

God's inspired words provide us wisdom and guidance on proper relationships we are to have, one to the other.

Knowing and Understanding Our Heritage

Also, in my opinion, in order for the African American community to become a community of healthy people, we must address our Africanists and embrace our heritage. We must accept who we are; realize we are a people of African descent, good, bad, or indifferent. We are not who and what others say we are. We are a spiritual people, whose foundation and roots are in Africa. We must identify with that spirit as well, as a means of healing and making us whole and complete again. We must realize that we are an African people; that our historic roots are deeper than the history of slavery that our people endured in this country. We have a country and continent or origin; we are African people, with a history beyond slavery and the Slave Trade. We must discover and learn to respect and love that history. History is the foundation of a people, it's the DNA of their cultural milieu; it makes them who they are.

Our forefathers came from a country rich in precious minerals and natural resources, a rich soil that will grow any and everything. We are of a linage of people that goes back to the time of creation. We come from a noble and spirit loving people. I speak of these things from a historic perspective so we can relate to our genetic composition as a people in this healing conversation, not just the chattel slavery experience of our people in this country where our people were treated as property, as less than human beings, owned by other men, to be sold and traded like livestock property, to do with as they pleased. We are more than the experience of slavery that our elders endured. We are a great and noble people. We must learn to love us.

There was a system in place called "seasoning" that was used to condition the men and women from Africa, to break them down, de-humanize them, and reduce them to sub-human status in their minds as well as in the minds of the white men who owned them as slaves, allowing them to justify the system. This was a form of conditioning that has affected the psyche of the whole world; we are the ones that must change this perception.

Along with this came the concept of "white supremacy and black inferiority." Jim Crow Laws stated that a "Black" man had no rights that a white man was bound to respect. This was done so a whole society of people could be condition to accept the reality of the sub-human African species that looked like humans, but were not. We were considered to be more ape-like than human-like. This is a perception that has never been addressed. We are no longer considered, "ape -like" but we are still considered sub-human being and inferior to

Europeans, or white folk if you will. We are the ones who must alter this distorted perception of reality of who we are.

My aim here is not to provide a historical overview of the history of slavery and the slave trade, but to elevate the conscious level of the healing conversation to recognize and realize the devastating impact the system of chattel slavery has had on shaping a world view of African people. The episode of slavery has had an altering effect on the psychological and spiritual wholesomeness of how African people view themselves. We must devise ways to rid ourselves of this intrusion and contamination of the invasion by Europeans and others into the continent of Africa. We have been infected as a people, culturally and spiritually, similar to how viruses, germs, bacteria, parasites invade the human body.

As a people we must rid ourselves of this disease and disorder and see ourselves as great and wonderful people, to make us healthy and whole again. This is the purpose of the healing conversation; to focus ourselves on ourselves. There is a saying that says, "Know thy self." There is another saying that says, "The truth shall set you free." That is what we are seeking in this conversation, to be free. We need to be free from this mental intrusion that has impacted our identity and relationships with our God and ourselves.

There has never been a counter-balancing force or action to address the mental and spiritual devastating effects of the Slave Trade. We must reconnect to who we are as an African People. We must embrace that we are a spiritual, loving, creative and noble people in order for the healing to begin.

Malcolm X once said, "We've been tricked, hoodwinked and bamboozled."

Spike Lee said, "Wake up." "Do the right thing."

Dr. Martin Luther King said, "The time is now."

I, Edgar L. Gosa say, "Let the healing begin. It starts with the love of God in our lives and the love of self."

What's Love Got to Do with It?

This is an apt opportunity to have a brief decision about "Love." What is love? How are we to relate to love? When is it appropriate for love; to give and receive love? Love is a serious and complicated endeavor, yet sweet and rewarding.

This is my take on the subject. I will start with what is presented in Webster's New World Dictionary. It defines love as:

- Strong affection or liking for someone or something

- A passionate affection of one person for another

- The object of such affection; a sweetheart or lover

Ponder this expression of love for a moment; it's very limited in scope. It points to a one-on-one love, not a group or collective love. Something to think about.

Is it possible to have group or collective love? Can we love everyone? I think so. All we have to do is follow God's plan.

The Bible has this to say:

By this shall all men know that ye are my disciples, if ye have love one to another.

John 13:35

But above all these things put on love, which is the bond of perfection.

Colossians 3:14 (NKJV)

Now the purpose of the commandment is love from a pure heart, from a good conscience, and from sincere faith,

1 Timothy 1:5 (NKJV)

Flee also youthful lusts; but pursue righteousness, faith, love, peace with those who call on the Lord out of a pure heart.

2 Timothy 2:22 (NKJV)

That the older men be sober, reverent, temperate, sound in faith, in love, in patience;

Titus 2:2 (NKJV)

Let brotherly love continue.

Hebrews 13:1

Beloved, let us love one another: for love is of God; and every one that loveth is born of God, and knoweth God. He that loveth not knoweth not God; for God is love.

1 John 4:7-8

Jesus said unto him, Thou shalt love the Lord thy God with all thy heart, and with all thy soul, and with all thy mind.

Matthew 22:37

This is the first and great commandment. And the second is like unto it, Thou shalt love thy neighbour as thyself.

Matthew 22:38-39

Meditate on these two perspectives of love and don't be biased toward the source. Concentrate on the validity and spirit of what is being offered. Open your mind and your heart, seeking an understanding and let love abound in you. Focus on what is good and wholesome for a people and commit to helping make it happen. I focus attention on the two sources with this comment. One is carnal in nature, which is individually directed. The other is spiritual in nature, which is collectively directed. Both have to do with love but notice there is a difference; whether it's individual or collective. The healing conversation is about recognizing this difference and applying a proper balance. They both have a place in our lives.

We must reconnect to our source of creation, which is Spirit, and from where we descended, which is what we know as Africa. A people must relate to who they are and where they are from. This provides them with roots and a foundation from which to grow. When I was growing up there were sayings like, "Deeper the roots, stronger the tree" and "The blacker berry, the sweeter the juice." As I reflect on them now, I can discern the wisdom in them as it relates to roots and foundation. I will end the conversation at this time with this. Let us relate to our roots and identify with our foundation so we can grow into a wholesome, healthy family of people.

Now that we have started, let's continue the dialogue. This conversation is far from over!

Endnote

Agreeing with me or not agreeing with me is not important, but having the conversation is. Look around our community, what do you see? Are there problematic issues that need to be addressed? Do you see a wholesome, viable, collective, loving group of people, working together toward improving their lot and that of their family, friends, and neighbors? Look at what's happening with the people that make up the community, ask yourself, your family and your friends, and don't leave out the children; is this a community that makes you proud? Is this a community that makes you feel safe and secure? Is this a community of people that makes you feel empowered? Or, is this a community that makes you feel alienated, disconnected and insecure? After an open, honest discussion and assessment of these concerns, if you don't see a community that is in need of healing, then this conversation is non-existent for you. You have nothing to add to the discussion of the need for healing. However, if you do see the need, then carry the conversation on, get involved; realizing it's up to each one of us to get focused and directed toward improving the situation and to do our personal part in making our community a better place in which to live.

On the pages of this book, I'm presenting a perspective that's unfolding to me and in me, bit by bit to be used as food for thought. I hope that it will help generate a focused conversation. Please understand that what is presented here is just a part of the remedy for the restoration and healing of a people to help make them whole again. I hope you find it stimulating and rewarding. It's all about Love!

Suggested Book Reading List:

The New Scofield Study Bible

The Africans Who Wrote the Bible; Nana Banchie Darkwah, Ph. D

Biblical History of Black Mankind; C. McGhee Livers

The Black Presence in The Bible; Rev. Walter Arthur McCray

Christianity Before Christ; John G. Jackson

The Destruction of Black Civilization; Chancellor Williams

The African Abroad; William Henry Ferris

Maat; Ra Un Nefer Amen

Metu Neter, Vol. 1; Ra Un Nefer Amen

Metu Neter, Vol. 2; Ra Un Nefer Amen

The Gift of Black Folk; W.E.B. Du Bois

On Sociology and the Black Community; W.E.B. Du Bois

W.E.B. Du Bois - A Profile; Rayford W. Logan

The Negro People - In American History; William Z. Foster

The Burden of Race; Gilbert Osofsky

Fulcrums of Change; Jan Carew

Black Culture – Theory and Practice; Amuzie Chimezie, Ph. D.

Message to the Blackman – In America; Elijah Muhammad

The Three Battlegrounds; Francis Frangipane

The Gospel of Inclusion – Bishop Carlton Pearson

Armageddon; Grant R. Jeffery

Rediscovering the Kingdom; Myles Munroe

The New Jim Crow; Michelle Alexander

The Psychopathic Racial Personality; Bobby E. Wright

Yurugu; Marimba Ani

They Stole It But You Must Return It; Richard Williams, Ed. D

Stolen Legacy; Asa G. Hilliard III

The Community of Self; Dr. Na'im Akbar

The Temple in Man; R. A. Schwaller de Lubicz

The Book of Coming Forth by Day; Maulana Karenga

Let the Circle be Unbroken; Dona Marimba Richards